D1243843

TREASURE HUNTERS

ANCIENT TREASURES

NICK HUNTER

Chicago, Illinois

Edited by Laura Knowles, Adam Miller, Harriet Milles, and Helen Cox Cannons
Designed by Victoria Allen
Original illustrations © Capstone Global Library Ltd 2013
Illustrated by Martin Bustamante
Picture research by Tracy Cummins

Originated by Capstone Global Library Ltd.
Production by Alison Parsons
Printed in the United States of America in North Mankato, Minnesota. 042013   007336RP

16 15 14 13
10 9 8 7 6 5 4 3

Library of Congress Cataloging-in-Publication Data

Hunter, Nick.
  Ancient treasures / Nick Hunter.
    p. cm.—(Treasure hunters)
  Includes bibliographical references and index.
  ISBN 978-1-4109-4950-9 (hb)—ISBN 978-1-4109-4957-8 (pb) 1. Treasure troves—Juvenile literature. 2. Civilization, Ancient—Juvenile literature. 3. Archaeology—History—Juvenile literature. I. Title.

  G525.H8974 2013
  930.1—dc23   2012012757

Acknowledgments

We would like to thank the following for permission to reproduce photographs: Alamy pp.5 bot (©North Wind Picture Archives), 7 bot (©Philip Game), 22 (©Picture Contact BV), 32 (©Peter Horree), 34 (©Robert Harding Picture Library Ltd); AP Photo p.14 (David Jones/PA Wire); Art Resources pp.23 (©The Trustees of the British Museum), 30 (bpk, Berlin/Kunstbibliothek, Staatliche Museen); British Museum p.13 (©The Trustees of the British Museum); Corbis pp.15 (©Eddie Keogh/Reuters), 24 (©Alfredo Dagli Orti/The Art Archive), 25 (©Radius Images), 28 (©West Semitic Research/Dead Sea Scrolls Foundation), 31 (©Bettmann); Getty Images pp.5 top (J.D. Dallet), 7 top (NYPL/Science Source), 26 (DEA PICTURE LIBRARY/De Agostini), 35 (MAURICIO DUENAS/AFP), 37 (Stock Montage), 40; istockphoto p.38 (©Evgeny Bashta); National Geographic p.17; Newscom pp.10 (akg-images), 16 (Photoshot), 20 (Jules Annan / Retna Pictures); Rex USA p. 11 top; Shutterstock pp.1 (Jiri Vaclavek), 4 left (Konstanttin), 4 right x 2 (Gordan Sermek), 4 right (I. Pilon), 6 (Anneka), 8 (David Hughes), 9 (Stocksnapper), 11 bot (Krivosheev Vitaly), 12 (Catalin Petolea), 21 top (kstudija), 21 bot (afoto6267), 27 (RYGER), 29 (Ella Hanochi), 32-33 (Santiago Cornejo), 36 (Juri), 39 (Ozerov Alexander), 41 bot (Tom Nance), 41 top (jamie Thorpe); Superstock p.43 (©Robert Harding Picture Library); THE KOBAL COLLECTION LUCASFILM LTD/PARAMOUNT p.42. Design features: Shutterstock.

Cover photographs reproduced with permission of Shutterstock ©Balefire/creativedoxfoto/inxti/Marques/Sergey856.

Expert consultant

We would like to thank Dr. Michael Lewis for his invaluable help in the preparation of this book. Dr. Lewis is deputy head of the Department of Portable Antiquities and Treasure at the British Museum, London.

Guided Reading Level: W

CONTENTS

THE SEARCH FOR TREASURE

History is full of stories of people searching for treasure and other precious objects from the past. History's treasure hunters range from the robbers who stole gold and other valuables from the tombs of ancient Egyptian kings to modern people using metal detectors to find artifacts buried hundreds of years ago.

From the 1400s onward, European explorers such as Christopher Columbus and Francis Drake sailed across oceans to find new lands. These pioneers were exploring for a reason. They wanted to find riches—both for themselves and those who sponsored them. Some found huge wealth and fame, while others died trying. The pursuit of treasure also destroyed whole civilizations, such as the Aztecs and Incas of Central and South America.

FEELING LUCKY?

Sometimes treasure hunters find what they are looking for, but at other times the treasures remain hidden—perhaps never to be found! Some people spend their lives searching for amazing finds that will give them a glimpse of how people lived in the past. Amazingly, people who were not even looking for them sometimes find the greatest treasures.

Ideas about treasure change over time. For European explorers in the 1500s, spices from the East were highly valued. In the days before refrigerators, spices could be used to make rotten meat taste a little better!

From the earliest civilizations, gold has been prized more than other metals.

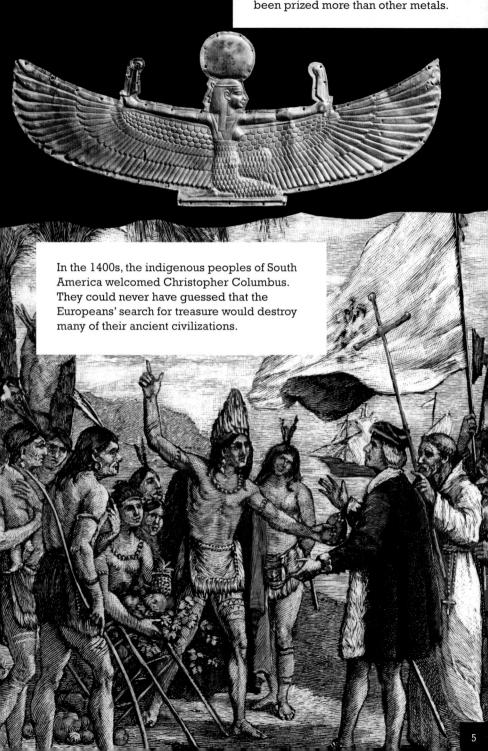

In the 1400s, the indigenous peoples of South America welcomed Christopher Columbus. They could never have guessed that the Europeans' search for treasure would destroy many of their ancient civilizations.

WHERE DOES TREASURE COME FROM?

Treasure can lie hidden or undiscovered for many reasons. Hundreds of years ago, most people did not have banks or safes to store their wealth. Instead, they hid money and valuables away from raiders or others who might try to steal it. This treasure was sometimes lost or never claimed by the people who hid it.

Sometimes treasure was hidden or collected on purpose—for example, as part of a religious offering. Many kings from ancient Egypt to Anglo-Saxon Britain were buried along with their most precious possessions, which they believed they would need in the afterlife.

Not all treasures are made of precious metals such as gold and silver. For archaeologists, the value of these finds lies in what they can tell us about the past--a time in history or a particular event.

Medieval alchemists tried to make their own treasure by attempting to turn base metals such as lead and iron into gold and silver. This was impossible, but the work of alchemists did lay some of the foundations for modern science.

Modern techniques for finding treasure

Many of the greatest treasures have been found since 1970. New technologies such as metal detectors, GPS, and sonar have helped those searching for archaeological objects. Without these, many great treasures would have never been found.

The Mildenhall Treasure is a collection of Roman silverware. It was discovered by accident in 1942 when a farmer was plowing his fields in Suffolk, England.

ROMAN RICHES

The year is 410 CE. For many centuries, Britain has been part of the Roman Empire. Now, the Roman army is leaving because it is needed to defend the city of Rome from barbarian invasion. The local people of Britain must now fend for themselves.

Throughout the 5th century, as the Romans begin to withdraw from Britain, new people from northwest Europe, including the Angles and Saxons, come to Britain.

"THE BARBARIANS PUSH US TO THE SEA; THE SEA PUSHES US BACK ON TO THE BARBARIANS. BETWEEN THESE TWO KINDS OF DEATH, WE ARE EITHER DROWNED OR SLAUGHTERED."

THE BRITONS' PLEA TO ROME FOR HELP TO FIGHT THE ANGLO-SAXONS, ACCORDING TO WRITING BY BEDE (c. 672–735)

Forts like this were not enough to deter the Anglo-Saxon raiders.

The Britons pleaded to Rome for help in fighting off the Anglo-Saxons, according to the monk Gildas (c. 500–570 CE). Gildas suggested the Anglo-Saxons used violence—destroying towns and land and killing Britons. Today, many archaeologists and historians believe that the Anglo-Saxon settlement of England was much more peaceful. Even so, these were uncertain times, and people who had wealth did what they could to protect it. Sometimes valuable possessions were hidden in the ground and collected later.

FABULOUS FIND

In 1992, close to the village of Hoxne in Suffolk, England, Eric Lawes was using his metal detector in a field near his home. He found one of the most remarkable treasures ever discovered in Britain.

Eric Lawes was actually using his metal detector to look for a local farmer's lost hammer when he discovered the Hoxne Hoard.

Secret Silver

Eric Lawes had discovered an astonishing collection of silver tableware, gold jewelry, and almost 15,000 gold, silver, and bronze coins of the Roman period. When he got a sense of how important his amazing find was, he did the right thing and contacted local archaeologists, so that they could study the site properly.

The Hoxne Hoard was probably buried sometime in the early 400s CE, around the time when the Roman army was leaving Britain. The coins and other treasures had been neatly packed in a wooden chest, although the chest had rotted over 1,600 years in the ground.

Whoever buried the hoard was a wealthy person and probably planned to come back for these precious things. But why did the person bury the box, and why did he or she never collect it?

This picture shows some of the first Anglo-Saxons arriving in Britain in the 5th century CE.

Slivers of silver had been clipped from the edges of many coins in the hoard. This silver may have been used to make new silver coins or other objects.

Metal detecting

Since the 1970s, metal detectors have helped amateur treasure hunters to make many important discoveries. The detector creates a magnetic field. When the field comes into contact with a metal object, it is disrupted, because the object becomes magnetized. The detector then makes a noise.

MYSTERIES OF THE HOARD

As the Romans withdrew from Britain and the future looked uncertain, the owners of the treasure may have decided that their valuables were not safe at home anymore. However, the hoard does not include any dishes or other large items, which a wealthy family would surely have owned. What happened to these things? Were they hidden elsewhere, or did they fall into the hands of looters?

Another mystery is the location where the treasure was found. Archaeologists have found no sign that it was close to a Roman villa or similar building. Perhaps the secret place was marked with a tree or a wooden post?

Clues

Do we know any more about the owners themselves? Buried with the hoard was a bracelet that was inscribed in Latin. It said, "Use this happily, Lady Juliane." Could Juliane have been the owner of the riches? The name Aurelius Ursicinus also appears on several objects. Eric Lawes unearthed not just treasure, but a priceless snapshot of life in the final days of the Roman Empire.

The Hoxne Hoard included four incredibly rare silver pepper containers (see below). For the Romans, pepper was almost as valuable as gold and silver. They had to bring it all the way from India. So, a family who could afford to fill four pepper containers was very wealthy.

"ABOUT 90 PERCENT OF ALL ARCHAEOLOGICAL FINDS FOUND IN ENGLAND AND WALES COME FROM PLOWED LAND. IN EFFECT, PEOPLE DOING METAL-DETECTING ARE RECOVERING THESE ITEMS BEFORE THEY'RE SMASHED TO BITS."

MICHAEL LEWIS,
BRITISH MUSEUM

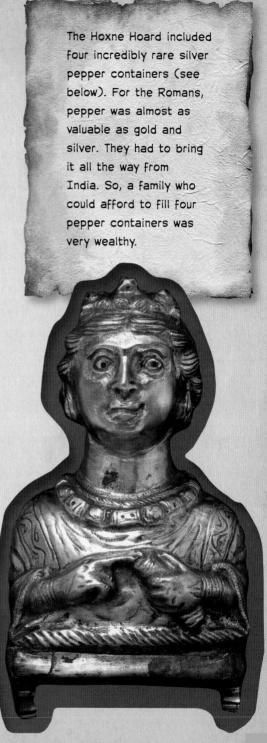

AMAZING ANGLO-SAXON DISCOVERY

In July 2009, Terry Herbert was metal detecting in a field in Staffordshire, England. His detector signaled that there was metal underground. Herbert thought he would just find more rusty old furniture hardware, as he had found elsewhere in the same field.

Herbert dug into the ground and pulled out an object that looked like brass. When he cleaned it off, Herbert realized with shock that it was gold!

As Herbert dug farther, the finds kept coming. They included parts of war equipment, including sword and helmet fragments, as well as Christian crosses decorated with red garnet gemstones. By the time he had finished, Herbert had uncovered one of the greatest treasures ever found, with more than 3,500 objects of gold and silver, many of which were in small pieces.

When Herbert realized the importance of his discovery, he alerted professional archaeologists. They excavated the spot and recovered important information about the find and clues to why it was buried.

TERRY HERBERT

Born: 1954

Nationality: British

Terry Herbert had been metal detecting for many years when he stumbled on the find of a lifetime. His discovery is now known as the Staffordshire Hoard.

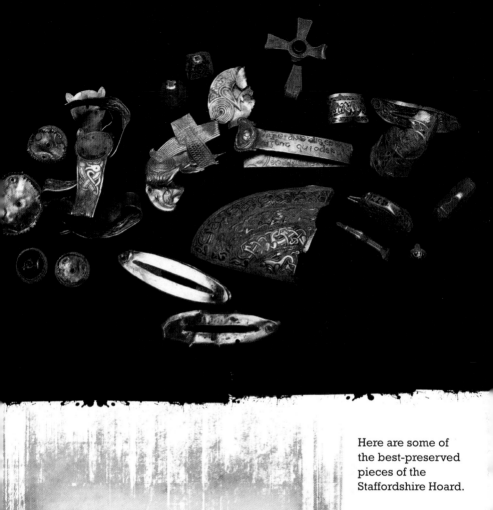

Here are some of the best-preserved pieces of the Staffordshire Hoard.

When Terry Herbert showed the six boxes of treasure he had collected to archaeologists, they were "virtually speechless" with excitement. Herbert shared the large reward for finding the hoard with the owner of the land, farmer Fred Johnson— as is required by British law.

A UNIQUE TREASURE

The Staffordshire Hoard was a unique discovery. Rather than a collection of coins or jewelry, it was almost completely made up of parts of weapons and military equipment, including 92 sword pommels. Many of the objects continue to baffle the archaeologists who are studying them.

DEADLY WEAPONS

From studying Anglo-Saxon skeletons, we know that the weapons of the time could easily split open a person's skull.

This gold sword pommel is decorated with garnets. The people who buried the hoard were only interested in gold and silver metals, not parts made of copper-alloy or iron.

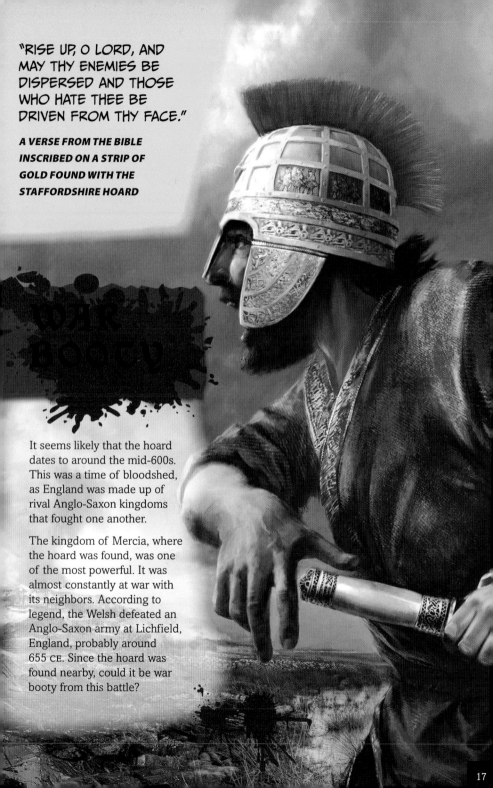

"RISE UP, O LORD, AND MAY THY ENEMIES BE DISPERSED AND THOSE WHO HATE THEE BE DRIVEN FROM THY FACE."

A VERSE FROM THE BIBLE INSCRIBED ON A STRIP OF GOLD FOUND WITH THE STAFFORDSHIRE HOARD

WAR BOOTY

It seems likely that the hoard dates to around the mid-600s. This was a time of bloodshed, as England was made up of rival Anglo-Saxon kingdoms that fought one another.

The kingdom of Mercia, where the hoard was found, was one of the most powerful. It was almost constantly at war with its neighbors. According to legend, the Welsh defeated an Anglo-Saxon army at Lichfield, England, probably around 655 CE. Since the hoard was found nearby, could it be war booty from this battle?

Burying the Staffordshire Hoard

cross

sword pommels

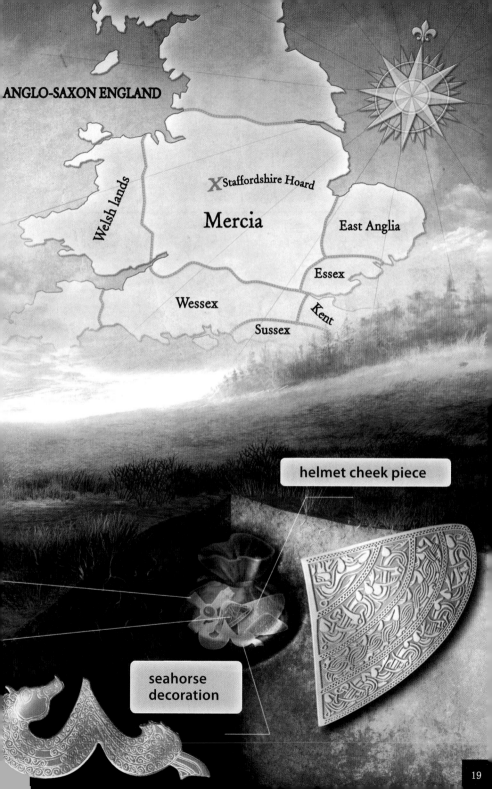

ANGLO-SAXON ENGLAND

X Staffordshire Hoard

Mercia

Welsh lands

East Anglia

Essex

Wessex

Kent

Sussex

helmet cheek piece

seahorse decoration

WHO AND WHY?

For so many weapons to be found together, someone must have collected them. Swords were a great status symbol for Anglo-Saxon warriors—they were created by skilled craftsmen and therefore cost a lot of money to produce. In Anglo-Saxon poems, swords are also celebrated for their magical powers.

Although the treasure includes many ornate sword hilts and pommels, there are no traces of the razor-sharp blades of the swords. Was the treasure hidden by the person who owned it, or was it looted from the dead of battle?

We know that some treasure is hidden to stop someone from stealing it, or just for safekeeping. But treasure could also be buried as a religious offering.

Some objects, such as this cross, show us that some of the treasure once belonged to a Christian.

THE DARK AGES

This period of history is often known as the Dark Ages because there are few written records to help us understand it. Archaeologists may never be able to answer all the questions about the Staffordshire Hoard, but there are many theories about this great historical mystery.

WULFHERE, KING OF MERCIA

Ruled from 657 to 675 CE

Wulfhere was a fierce warrior who became the most powerful king in southern Britain. Perhaps the Staffordshire Hoard could have belonged to Wulfhere, or he could have captured it from his enemies. If the treasure belonged to Wulfhere, why did he or his successors not claim it?

The Staffordshire Hoard was only just below the surface, and Terry Herbert was not the first person to search for archaeological objects in this field. It seems amazing that the treasure had been undiscovered for 1,300 years.

X-ray investigation

The latest technology was used to find out more information about the hoard. A process called X-ray fluorescence could study the metals in the hoard without damaging the treasures. Researchers found that the gold in some objects was much purer than that used in modern jewelry. Experts also examined the garnets in the hoard, which could have come from as far away as India.

Was the treasure buried to hide it? If so, why did no one ever come back for it? One possible explanation is that the burial was to give thanks for a victory over enemies.

SPOILS OF WAR

The contents of the hoard give us clues about why it was collected together in the first place. These were probably the spoils of war, gathered by a victorious army. The sword pommels and other items were not just from ordinary soldiers. These were elite forces, possibly the guard for a king or lord, who were armed with the finest weapons available. The razor-sharp blades of the swords were not part of the treasure. Instead, this metal may have been melted down to make into new weapons.

No one can be sure of the hoard's story, but we can admire the skill of the craftspeople who made the objects and also understand a bit more about the life of an Anglo-Saxon warrior.

The hoard was valued at more than $5 million! It included 11 pounds (5 kg) of gold and 5.5 pounds (2.5 kg) of silver. But its historical worth was much greater than the value of the metals used.

SECRETS OF THE ANCIENTS

Many of the world's greatest treasures are not made of gold or silver. Instead, they are often made of incredibly fragile materials. They are valuable because they are sacred to a religion, or because they give us a view of the world and history that we could not get from anywhere else.

Treasures can include historical documents or artifacts. One of the most important and valuable documents ever discovered was actually written on a stone. It enabled modern scholars to unlock the secrets of a whole civilization that lasted for more than 3,000 years.

There was no great hunt or expedition to find the Rosetta Stone. Like many of the greatest treasures, it was discovered by accident.

The Rosetta Stone held the key to hieroglyphs, the alphabet of ancient Egypt.

UNLOCKING ANCIENT EGYPT

The Rosetta Stone does not look much like treasure, since it is not gold. It is a black granite stone with an inscription in three different languages. It is this inscription that makes it priceless, because the three languages say the same thing three times—in ancient Greek, in the everyday language of ancient Egypt, and in the complex hieroglyphic writing used by the ancient Egyptians on formal occasions. Scholars could use the ancient Greek inscription to decipher the Egyptian hieroglyphs that had been a mystery for hundreds of years.

OUT OF EGYPT

The Rosetta Stone was discovered in 1799 by Pierre-François Bouchard, a French soldier on an expedition in Egypt, serving in the army of the French leader Napoleon. When the British army defeated French forces in 1801, they took possession of the stone and other ancient objects. The stone was taken back to London in triumph, where it was put on public display in the British Museum.

Although the Rosetta Stone was on display, it took 20 years to unravel the secrets of hieroglyphs. In the end, it was a Frenchman named Jean-François Champollion, building upon the work of others, who solved the mystery. Decoding hieroglyphs was the most important step in understanding the ancient civilization of Egypt. Now it was possible for those exploring the pyramids and the royal tombs in the Valley of the Kings to find out much more about the mysteries and treasures of ancient Egypt.

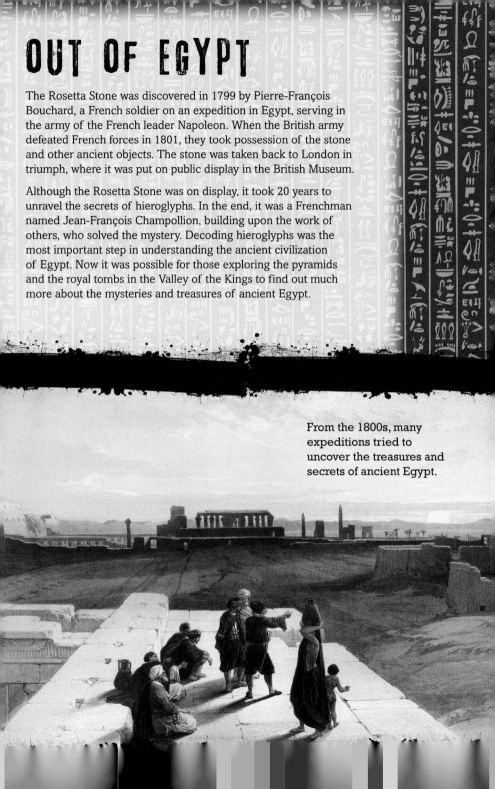

From the 1800s, many expeditions tried to uncover the treasures and secrets of ancient Egypt.

JEAN-FRANÇOIS CHAMPOLLION

Born: 1790

Died: 1832

Nationality: French

Champollion was a brilliant student who had learned 12 languages by the age of 16, and another 12, including Latin and Greek, by the time he was 20. He became a teacher, but he was dedicated to solving the riddle of hieroglyphs.

Cracking the code

The Rosetta Stone was a fascinating puzzle for the world's finest minds. British scientist Thomas Young figured out that a series of symbols that appeared several times were the name of the Egyptian king Ptolemy. Jean-François Champollion was the man who actually cracked the code, when he figured out that hieroglyphs could represent a mixture of sounds and whole words.

THE DEAD SEA SCROLLS

In 1947, a young shepherd tending his goats at Qumran, on the west bank of the Dead Sea, stumbled upon a series of ancient scrolls bound up with leather and hidden in a cave. These fragile treasures were one of the most important archaeological discoveries of all time. As people realized what the shepherd had unearthed, archaeologists searched other caves in the area and discovered many more documents.

The scrolls had lain undisturbed in their caves for around 2,000 years. They were hidden there by a Jewish religious community—possibly during the Jewish Revolt against Roman rule in 66 CE. In addition to including a complete version of the Old Testament of the Bible, the scrolls shone a light on the history of two of the world's great religions—Judaism and Christianity.

There are over 50,000 pieces of the Dead Sea Scrolls, which are the remains of more than 800 manuscripts.

Like many treasures, there has been a dispute over the scrolls' ownership: they are claimed by both Jordan and Israel. But images of the scrolls can now be viewed online, so that people around the world can see them.

Radiocarbon dating

To find out the age of a historic object and whether it is genuine, archaeologists sometimes use radiocarbon dating. This tests the levels of a form of carbon in things that were once living, such as wood or plant products. The level of carbon changes as the material becomes older. Radiocarbon dating found that the Dead Sea Scrolls dated from between 150 BCE and 70 CE.

This is the region of Qumran where the scrolls were found in caves.

TREASURES OF THE NEW WORLD

One of the biggest hunts for treasure in history lasted for hundreds of years and cost many millions of innocent lives. It began in the late 1400s with the voyages of Christopher Columbus from Spain to the New World of the Americas. Adventurers such as Hernán Cortés and Francisco Pizarro continued the search for new lands and treasure in the Americas. These treasure hunters were known as *conquistadors* (conquerors).

In 1519, Cortés led an expedition to the great Aztec Empire, in what is now Mexico. When the Spanish saw the splendor of the Aztec capital, Tenochtitlán, they knew that the Aztecs and their leader, Montezuma, had the gold and silver they wanted. In the years that followed, they conquered the Aztecs. Aztec gold and silver was transported to Spain, although there are still many stories of lost treasures hidden at the time of the invasion.

Aztec weapons were no match for the guns and horses of the Spanish invaders.

In 1531, Francisco Pizarro and his brothers set out with around 200 men to conquer Peru. Spurred on by reports of fabulous treasure, they headed inland to the city of Cajamarca. There they met the Inca leader, Atahualpa (see next page).

FRANCISCO PIZARRO

Born: 1475

Died: 1541

Nationality: Spanish

Pizarro was one of the most successful and the cruelest of the Spanish conquistadors. He discovered the Inca Empire and founded the city of Lima. But he would stop at nothing in his search for treasure and power—including the murder of Inca leader Atahualpa and many others.

There are many myths about buried treasure belonging to Emperor Montezuma. Some say it remains buried beneath modern Mexico City, which stands on the site of the Aztec capital.

LOST INCA GOLD

When Atahualpa arrived with thousands of unarmed supporters, Pizarro's men attacked them and murdered more than 2,000 people. Atahualpa was captured, and Pizarro agreed to release him in return for a room full of gold. Part of the ransom was delivered, but Pizarro double-crossed the Incas and had Atahualpa strangled. The location of the rest of Atahualpa's ransom is still a mystery.

The Incas could not understand the Spanish obsession with gold. Gold decoration was very important to them, and it was given as a gift, but they never used gold as money.

MOUNTAIN LEGEND

Legend says that the treasure was hidden away in the mountains of Ecuador. The main source of this legend is a Spanish adventurer named Valverde, who claimed to have been shown the treasure.

For centuries, many explorers have followed Valverde's written directions to try to find the treasure, but none had succeeded. Maybe it is still out there, hidden in the jungles of South America— or maybe the treasure was never there at all?

American Barth Blake claimed to have found the treasure in 1886. In a letter, he said that he saw "thousands of gold and silver pieces of Inca and pre-Inca handicraft, the most beautiful goldsmiths' works you could imagine." But he could only take home as much as he could carry. On his return journey to New York to organize an expedition, he apparently fell overboard and was never seen again. Was he murdered? If so, the location of the treasure was lost with him.

THE TREASURE OF LAKE GUATAVITA

One story that fired the imagination of Spanish *conquistadors* looking for gold was the ceremony that the Muisca people of Lake Guatavita (in present-day Colombia) performed when a new ruler came to power.

According to the legend, a new ruler would be covered in gold dust and put on a raft loaded with other golden treasures. The raft would float out into the middle of the lake, where the gold would be thrown into the water as an offering to the Guatavita goddess.

The first Spanish explorers tried to drain the lake. In three months, they only lowered the water level by 9 feet (3 meters), but they found enough gold to convince people that the lake held a fabulous treasure.

The Spaniards had a name for the figure covered in gold--El Dorado, or "the golden one." This has come to be used for any mythical place where gold and riches can supposedly be found.

This model shows the ceremony of Lake Guatavita. The Spanish never actually saw the ceremony, as it is believed to have ended before they discovered the lake.

"WHEN THE RAFT REACHED THE CENTER OF THE LAGOON, THEY RAISED A BANNER AS A SIGNAL FOR SILENCE. THE GILDED INDIAN THEN ... [THREW] OUT ALL THE PILE OF GOLD INTO THE MIDDLE OF THE LAKE, AND THE CHIEFS WHO HAD ACCOMPANIED HIM DID THE SAME."

DESCRIPTION OF WHAT HAPPENED AT LAKE GUATAVITA, FROM A LETTER BY JUAN RODRIGUES FREYLE

GOLD DOWN THE DRAIN

Although the first Spanish explorers had not drained the lake, they had proved that the stories were true. Who would be the first to claim the entire treasure of Lake Guatavita?

In 1580, Antonio Supúlveda came up with an ingenious plan. He employed thousands of workers to dig a channel that would drain the lake. He managed to lower the water level by 66 feet (20 meters) and to claim a big haul of treasure. However, the project ended in disaster when the channel collapsed, killing many of the workers.

STUCK IN THE MUD

The most successful project began in 1911. A team led by Hartley Knowles dug a tunnel that would drain the lake from the middle, like a drain plug hole in a sink. Filters would catch any treasure that drained out with the water. But when the lake was drained, it left mud and slime about 5 feet (1.5 meters) deep. They were now within touching distance of the treasure, but the hot sun baked the mud on the bed of the lake until it was as hard as concrete. Most of the treasure was stuck beneath it, just beyond reach. Some gold was collected from the sides of the lake but, once again, Lake Guatavita defeated those seeking treasure.

British adventurer Walter Raleigh was another treasure hunter who led an expedition to South America in search of El Dorado.

"AS TO WHAT IS STILL THERE, THERE IS NO WAY OF FINDING OUT EXCEPT TO GO ON WITH THE DIGGING. CERTAINLY [THE CEREMONY] WENT ON FOR 200 YEARS. SO YOU SEE A GOOD DEAL MUST HAVE PILED UP."

TREASURE HUNTER HARTLEY KNOWLES, FROM AN INTERVIEW WITH THE NEW YORK TIMES IN 1912

UNDISCOVERED TREASURES

Amazing treasure finds like the Staffordshire Hoard show that there are treasures out there, under the ground, waiting to be found.

However, many legends about treasure are either untrue, or the details have been lost over the centuries. The idea that treasure is buried on a desert island is one of the greatest treasure myths. It is rarely true, but those looking for treasure may risk everything in the hope of finding untold riches.

TREASURE ISLAND

One such story tells of hundreds of barrels of treasure that were buried by a Spanish navigator on Juan Fernández Island in the Pacific Ocean. Many people have attempted to find the treasure, including American millionaire Bernard Keiser, who spent millions of dollars trying to do so.

In 2005, media around the world reported a breakthrough. The location of 600 barrels of treasure had been found. The company responsible said it had used ground-penetrating radar to find them. However, it soon became clear that they were not prepared to spend millions excavating the treasure. It seemed the world's media were the victims of a hoax.

Environmental impact

Juan Fernández Island is a World Biosphere Reserve, meaning that its plants and animals are protected and large-scale excavation is not allowed. However, Bernard Keiser has not given up. In 2010, he applied to use sophisticated mining equipment to search for treasure without disturbing the island's wildlife.

Juan Fernández Island is also known as Robinson Crusoe Island. This is because Daniel Defoe based his story of a stranded sailor, *Robinson Crusoe*, on Alexander Selkirk, who was abandoned on this island by his shipmates.

MODERN TREASURE HOARDS

Many lost or hidden treasures are far from the romantic desert islands of our imaginations. Treasures like the Hoxne Hoard were hidden at times of crisis. More recent conflicts have also featured their own stories of lost and buried treasure.

Gold and other treasures were discovered underground following the defeat of Nazi Germany in 1945.

NAZI GOLD

During World War II (1939–1945), Nazi Germany invaded many European countries and sent millions of Jews and others to their deaths in concentration camps. As they rampaged across the continent, Adolf Hitler's Nazi armies stole gold and other valuables from countries and individuals. They used the loot to pay for the war. After the war, more than 300 tons of gold were recovered, but experts believe there is more still to be found.

SECRETS OF THE LAKE

Many treasure seekers believe that the Nazis dumped gold into the isolated Lake Toplitz, high in the mountains of Austria. Many have tried to find the treasure. An unlucky few even lost their lives in the deep and treacherous waters. In 2009, the Austrian government announced a ban on diving in the lake. Although the Nazis certainly dumped weapons and fake money in the lake, no gold has been found.

In 1959, a team of treasure hunters found $113 million of British cash in Lake Toplitz. Sadly for them, the bills were forgeries created by the Nazis during World War II.

"EACH YEAR WE'RE CATCHING AT LEAST TEN DIVERS WHO COME HERE HOPING TO DISCOVER THE NAZI FORTUNE, EVEN THOUGH IT IS STRICTLY FORBIDDEN."

BERNHARD SCHRAGL, AUSTRIAN OFFICIAL, ON THE LURE OF LAKE TOPLITZ

FINDING TREASURE

Many legendary treasures do not exist or will never be found. However, people keep searching in the hope that one day they will find something as exciting and important as the Staffordshire Hoard.

If you are hunting for ancient artifacts, you need to accept that most days you will find nothing. But if you keep going, follow clues, and search in the right places, you might just find something that has been hidden for hundreds of years. You may even want to consider a career as an archaeologist.

Movies about hunting for hidden treasures rarely mention the many days when nothing is found!

Archaeology technology

Archaeologists use complex tools such as ground-penetrating radar and magnetometers to identify which parts of a site can be excavated. For the actual digging, they use common tools such as shovels. They use filters and toothbrushes to be sure they do not miss any important clues in the soil they remove.

"Nighthawks" are thieves who use their metal detectors to search for treasure on known archaeological sites. They often work at night so they do not get caught, but the police are getting much better at catching them.

DO THE RIGHT THING

If you are lucky enough to discover buried treasure or something very old, make sure you do the right thing. Report all your finds to make sure archaeologists get the chance to learn more about them or explore the site. Coins and other artifacts can tell amazing stories about how people lived in the past. You never know what they might reveal.

TIMELINE

196 BCE

The Rosetta Stone is inscribed by ancient Egyptian priests in three languages.

66 CE

The Jewish Revolt against Roman rule begins. This is likely when the Dead Sea Scrolls are hidden in a cave at Qumran, near the Dead Sea.

410

Roman legions leave Britain. Around this time, the Hoxne Hoard of coins and valuables is buried in Suffolk, England.

655

The Battle of Lichfield likely occurs between the Anglo-Saxons and Welsh.

1492

Christopher Columbus crosses the Atlantic Ocean and is the first European to discover the Americas. Columbus's voyage marks the start of the Spanish conquest of Central and South America.

1519

Hernán Cortés leads the first expedition to the capital of the Aztec Empire at Tenochtitlán.

1531

Francisco Pizarro begins the conquest of Peru and the Inca Empire, seizing large amounts of gold and silver for Spain.

1799

The Rosetta Stone is uncovered by French soldiers in Egypt.

1821-1822

Jean-François Champollion solves the mystery of Egyptian hieroglyphs, using the Rosetta Stone.

1942

The Mildenhall Treasure of Roman silverware is found buried in Suffolk, England.

1945

World War II ends in defeat for Nazi Germany. The search begins for gold and other treasures stolen by the Nazis.

1947

The Dead Sea Scrolls are discovered in a cave in Qumran, Palestine, by a young shepherd.

1992

The Hoxne Hoard is found with a metal detector by Eric Lawes in Suffolk, England.

2009

Terry Herbert uncovers the Staffordshire Hoard in a field in Staffordshire, England.

GLOSSARY

alchemist scientist from the medieval period. Alchemists tried to turn base metals into gold and silver.

Anglo-Saxon name used to describe the invaders and settlers who came to Britain from northern Europe from the 4th century CE, including Angles, Saxons, and Jutes

archaeologist person who studies the past by unearthing and examining historical remains

artifact anything made by humans, particularly something from the past

civilization society where people live in settled communities and have a certain culture or way of life

conquistador adventurers, such as Hernán Cortés, who led the Spanish invasion of the Americas in the 1500s

Dark Ages historical period after the decline of Roman Britain, about which we know little about because there are very few detailed written records

decipher solve a puzzle or crack a code

double-cross trick someone or go back on an agreement

elite people who are special or superior within a group or society

excavation archaeological dig

fragment small, broken piece

garnet red, semiprecious stones used for decoration

GPS (global positioning system) device that uses satellite signals to pinpoint the user's exact position

ground-penetrating radar radar that can detect objects hidden underground

hieroglyph character used in the writing system of ancient Egypt

hilt handle of a sword

hoax trick or forgery

indigenous first people to live in a certain place

inscription words or symbols carved into a stone or other object

Latin language used in ancient Rome and across the Roman Empire

magnetic field area around a magnet where magnetic forces have an effect

magnetometer piece of equipment that uses magnets to detect metals— for example, on the seabed

metal detector machine that can detect the presence of metal underground

ornate richly decorated—for example, with carvings or jewels

pommel decorative knob at the end of a sword handle

radiocarbon dating technique used to find out when an object was first made

ransom money demanded by criminals for the safe return of a person or object

sonar using sound waves to detect or map something under water

spoils treasure taken from an enemy during war

sponsor person who supports or provides money for something

X-ray fluorescence technique that uses X-rays to find out what historical objects are made of

FIND OUT MORE

Books

Adams, Simon. *Archaeology Detectives* (Uncovering the Past). Hauppauge, N.Y.: Barron's, 2009.

Gruber, Beth, and Johan Reinhard. *Ancient Inca: Archaeology Unlocks the Secrets of the Inca's Past* (National Geographic Investigates). Washington, D.C.: National Geographic, 2007.

Malam, John. *The Terracotta Army and Other Lost Treasures* (Lost and Found). Irvine, Calif.: QEB, 2011.

Spilsbury, Louise, and Richard Spilsbury. *History Detectives: Archaeologists* (Scientists at Work). Chicago: Heinemann Library, 2008.

Steele, Philip. *Treasure* (Eyewitness). New York: Dorling Kindersley, 2010.

Web sites

kids.nationalgeographic.com/kids/stories/history/ten-cool-sites/
Read about more archaeological sites at this web site.

www.nps.gov/archeology/public/kids/index.htm
Learn more about different kinds of archaeologists and what they do at this U.S. National Park Service web site.

science.nationalgeographic.com/science/archaeology
National Geographic's Archaeology web site features stories about amazing treasures and the latest discoveries.

www.unmuseum.org/nazigold.htm
Read more facts and stories about the search for treasure stolen by the Nazis during World War II.

Places to Visit

The American Museum of Natural History
Central Park West at 79th Street
New York, New York, 10024-5192
www.amnh.org
The American Museum of Natural History is home to many of the world's
greatest historical treasures, including archaeological finds from Egypt
and Latin American civilizations such as the Inca.

Smithsonian National Museum of Natural History
10th Street and Constitution Avenue, NW
Washington, D.C. 20560
www.mnh.si.edu
The National Museum of Natural History has archaeological finds from
many of the civilizations mentioned in this book and more.

Find out about local archaeological groups or news of archaeological
digs happening near your home. Contact them to see if you can visit
or find out more about their projects.

Topics for Further Research

Pick a historical treasure that really interests you and find out everything
you can about it. How was it made? Who would have used it? What does
it tell us about the past?

Discover more about the work of archaeologists. What techniques and
technology do they use to find out about the past? You could interview
some real archaeologists to find out about their work.

Explore the civilizations of Central and South America that were destroyed
by treasure seekers from Europe. What can you find out about the Inca
civilization of Peru? Why did the European invaders destroy civilizations
such as the Incas and the Aztecs?

INDEX